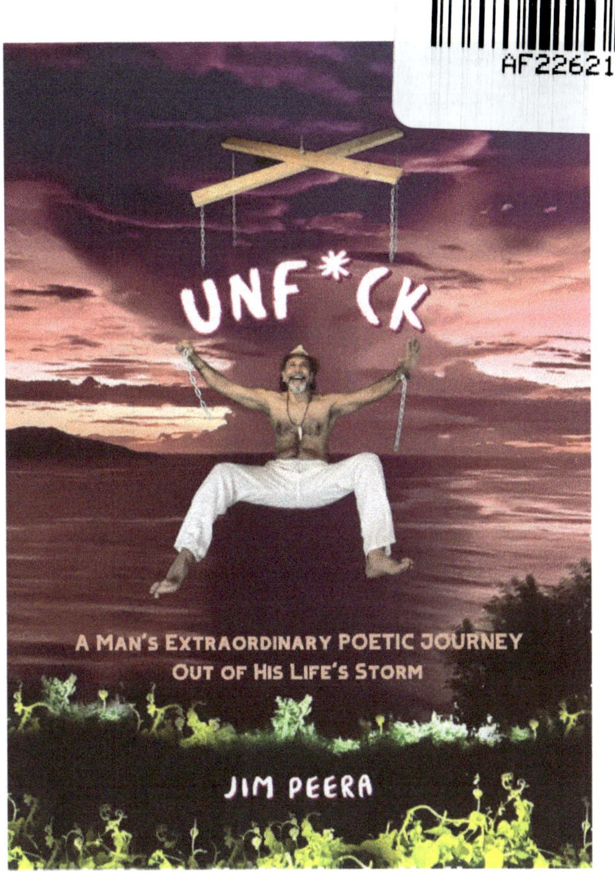

JIM PEERA

ISBN: 978-1-7375950-4-5

Printed in the United States of America

Dedicated to all those who have loved hard, been ripped apart with a mindfuck breakup and then thought:

"What the *fuck* now?"

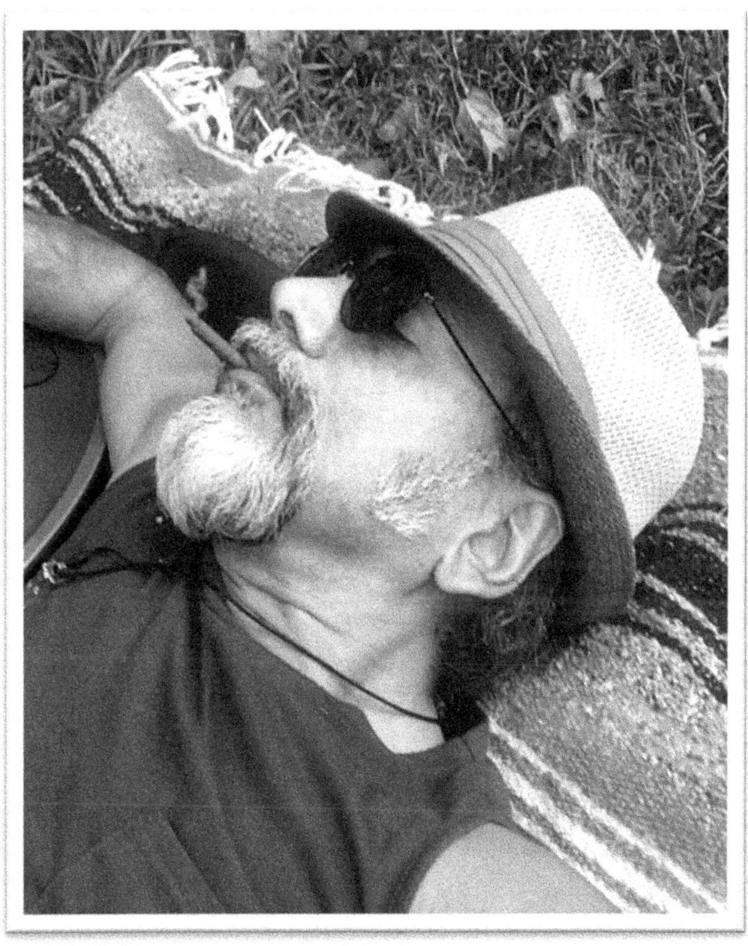

Selfie by Jim Peera

Table of Contents

"It's bad enough that you lose someone who's been a big part of your life and you've loved. But it's a tragedy to lose someone who you must love above all – and that is *YOU*."

- Jim Peera

Prologue

I remember quite vividly the WTF moment of my adult life.

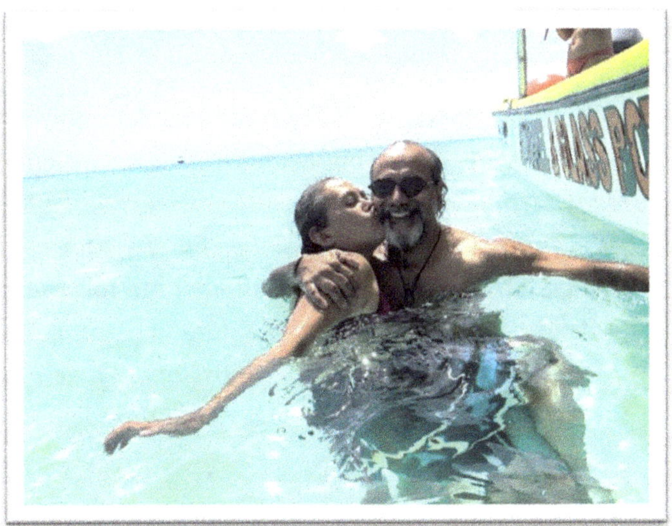

Earth Date: 08.02.2022

The daylight has just broken through the window curtains at a boutique hotel in Isla Holbox, Mexico. My beautiful and loving wife of forty years and I were winding down our amazing two-week vacation in the turquoise blue waters of the Mayan Riviera. We'd also just checked off our newest bucket list, Chichen Itza!

We now had only two days of paradise left before we headed back to our home in Atlanta, Georgia. *"Wow, isn't this an amazing life we're having honey! Did you ever dream we'd be doing all these adventures?"* She asked me. *"Yes, I always knew I'd be rich one day and have an exciting life with you."* I replied, as I kissed her while sailing on a chartered wind-powered catamaran.

That starlit night I was feeling pretty sexy and ready to ignite some passionate fire with the love of my life. But she said she was *"not in the mood"* again, and we fell asleep arguing about sex and a passing comment I made about her gaining a few pandemic pounds that wasn't digested well at all. So, I knew through the restless night that the morning would arrive looking like a black skull stuffed with a fiery jalapeno for me — ready to celebrate the Mexican Day of The Dead. And sadly, I was dead right!

My wife woke me up by nudging my shoulder while I was still asleep and said with a sad but wide-eyed stare into my squinty eyes *"Honey, I think I know why I'm not sexually pleasing you lately. I don't want to die living a lie, but I believe I am gay."* My eyes dilated as the morning sun blinded me for a second and I shook my head to reply *"WTF? no fucking way, that's impossible as you wouldn't have enjoyed making passionate love to me for 40 years! So, NO you are definitely not a closet gay. You're probably just a 'bi' honey."*

She then looked up to the adobe ceiling in a pensive gaze and seemed to not disagree with my assessment of her life's deep untold secret. In that moment, it jolted in me an old memory of the song by the musical group, Gap Band; 'You Dropped a Bomb on Me.' It was one of my wife's favorite tunes when we first met in Tucson, Arizona in 1981, when she was 18 and I was 20.

The little voice in my head wondered if this revelation was a mindfuck omen. For sure it was so disturbing that it had me dive into the shallow waters and want to drown to forget about the whole incident!

My wife who was sitting at the beach café sipping a strong cup of cappuccino must have felt my capsized heart sink to the bottom of the seabed as she pointed her cellphone towards the picturesque beach and snapped two photographs of me in emotional distress:

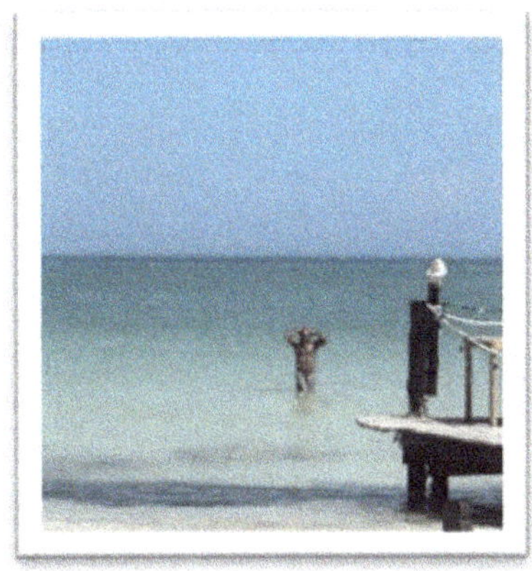 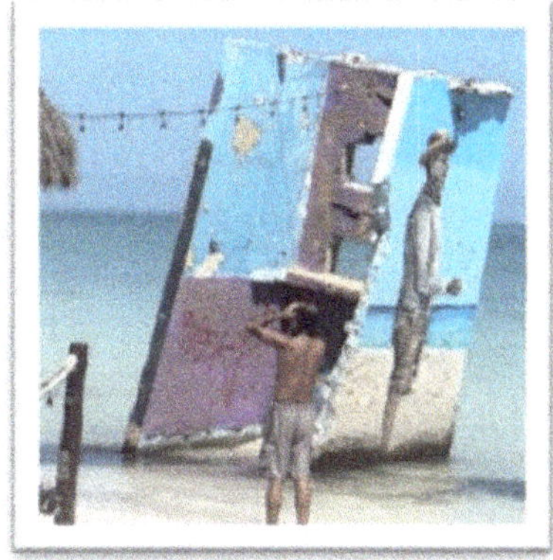

Earth Date: 08.09.2022

"Are you OK?", she asked as I returned to the table. *"Hell no, so what the fuck now?"* I responded in tears. Her answer was crystal clear as the Gulf of Mexico behind me. *"I feel so liberated right now and I'm sure you are too, being able to see anyone you want…and have sex with. Hey, we'll still be together and it can be like an 'open-relationship' that these kids have today!"* I was stunned by her nonchalant reply and asked if she was seeing anyone and having an affair. She refuted that question with a strong denial; *"No I am not!"* reassuring me how she's always been a loyal wife for four decades. And to this day I believe this truth. OK, so I thought to myself, this can't be that bad, or the end of the world. I then began to reassess the whole episode as a "progressive stage" in both our lives. We mutually agreed that we'd see a couple's therapist back home and figure the new arrangement out.

But things didn't go as planned, as she decided to attend a Native Indian sweat lodge and release some unhealed emotional cuts from her teenage years with a PTSD father and her oppressive upbringing. These old wounds reopened after the Covid-19 related death of her mother, who never acknowledged it while she was alive. Since we're all a product of our upbringing and present environment, my wife was sandwiched between her unsavory past and misandry influences among her circle of women friends. As the emotionally strongest, and closest male in her life, I've always helped cushion her pain with unconditional love. But now I was about to experience the wrath of the most unexpected personal storm heading in my direction. It began festering inside my wife's head quietly, and upon her return from the sweat she was distant with me and seemed to magnify all my negatives; past and present. Nothing I did or said was right as she blamed me for all the dirty dishes in the kitchen sink. My woman of light was in a dark place and I was the eye of the storm's landing site.

The future also seemed shaky as she returned from the therapist angry and wanted to take off to the mountains on her own to *"think things over,"* as she put it. I agreed that some time away would be good for both of us. So, she left me for two weeks but upon her return, my wife was much worse in her demeanor. The bouquets of red roses and sunflowers I bought to welcome her back were met with an uncanny mild "thank you," as an arrow dipped in fire was already pointing at my heart. I remember this date: **09.19.2022**

In my 61 years on this earth, this day for me was to become the most heartbreaking and mindfucking day of my adult life. And unless you've been happily married to someone for a long time, and either lost that person to a divorce or death, one has no damn reference point to compare! So, I realized right away that although many in my tiny close circle of friends, acquaintances, and family may know how to sympathize and console me — they couldn't truly empathize with my situation. This truth left me to grieve, cope and process it alone. This day was so gut-wrenching that it unleashed in me the first poem in this book, '*Dead or Alive.*'

My 59-year young wife, a gifted energy healer and a Western Shaman, proceeded to tell me that her power animal, the groundhog had confirmed to her twice; once at the sweat lodge and for the second time in the mountains, to set herself free of me and to leave me. But this wasn't a caged bird who had been grieving or unhappy at all. Ours was as authentic, strong and fun-loving of marriages as they come! So, I knew it wasn't about me. But her new perception became a reality and she pulled the bow and fired an arrow through my heart without hesitation, "*You're not going like what I have to say now, but I want to be by myself. I don't love you anymore and I think its best that we get a divorce.*"

To make matters worse, she had just filled out a therapist's '*getting to know your spouse*' questionnaire that both of us had to answer, and rated me 'very dissatisfied' in *all* aspects of the marriage. I on the other hand rated her near the 'highly satisfied' scale.

As any normal human would react to this falsity, I threw a fit, lost control of my emotions and told her that she was under some spell and had lost her head! "*Will my real wife wake up? What entity has entered your body to flip upside down on me?*" I shouted at her standing a few feet away, as I was weeping and wiping tears off my face and trying to make sense of this crisis. But her double-bladed arrow was not coated with any degree of trepidation. She had made up her mind and started packing. By the time both my children had arrived to witness the commotion, my wife had moved most of her belongings into her car to move out. And then the door slammed shut and my life partner was gone! I felt angry, perplexed and fucked.

The ensuing few nights were the longest of my life. Each day was excruciating for the mind, body and soul as I drank more alcohol, smoked many cigars and took cannabinoid edibles to cope with my new "surreality." I was a shattered man bleeding internally.

What did I do? What didn't I do? What the hell had just happened to my healthy and happy 40-year marriage that manifested in my life's storm? These were all questions tormenting me every painful minute that passed. But as the author of my first book *'The Healium Way'*, and a highly creative person, I knew I had to turn my lemons into margaritas and deploy my life's motto: *'Every problem has a creative solution.'*

I realized at the onset that in the worst-case scenario, even if we could not work things out and I lost my wife to the last resort 'divorce' outcome, that I couldn't afford to lose myself in the process. This truth and self-awareness became my catalyst to rebalance and not fall prey to many unhealthy ordinary trappings. I had to activate the 'extraordinary' human in me. By reducing the typical external *'feel good'* crutches to heal, find peace, and regain my power, I had to deploy the one therapeutic drug that always uplifts me and has never let me down; the medicine of the creative and healing arts. It's not just sound healing, drumming, sculpting, photography, dancing yoga, meditation, music, painting, — all my favorites that have helped me during my roughest ordeals in life. But this time I doubled down on expressing my sea of emotions and trauma through the unfiltered lens of POETRY.

The first three weeks following the breakup were the most difficult. My grieving took a toll on my sleep as I'd wake up around 4 A.M many mornings with dark emotions pouring out of me incessantly. Over half of the poems flowed out during this period and all were written in just two months. None have been sanitized or edited to keep it all real and raw for you, the reader.

This one word, *'unfuck'* kept ringing in my newly hijacked brain with an image of me cutting my own controlling strings of attachment causing my suffering; fear, ego, judgment and all the man-made low-vibration energy. It's the most suitable title for this book.

Each one of us six billion humans on this planet will experience some type of a personal heartbreak before we die. All breakups are mutually hard, especially for the unprepared receiver. But how we each deal with them is the key. During this dark breakdown period, we must go deep within ourselves before expecting any light to crack for a breakthrough.

These poems take you through my own trans-formative tunnel and are listed in the order of their real-time creation. They pack an emotional punch from pain to forgiveness and will captivate and entertain you "inteliciously" from start to finish. I know the mind-blasting exclusive video on page 23 will be a talking point. So, be sure to cast it on a large screen with friends if possible. It is my hope that you too will be inspired to use the medicine of creativity to unfuck yourself, as I've done for myself. So, let's get started!

Dead or Alive

I must confess I'm grieving like she's dead
Just can't get that damn woman out of my head

I know that old priest said 'until death do us part'
He lied, as I'm the one dying with her arrow through my heart

Every minute without her feels like a drowning hour
Sobbing and crying akin to an old leaky shower

We're all easily replaceable the therapists say
Explain that to my hard head that's gone astray

Having a lifelong soul partner is really awesome
Until it's abruptly cut short, leaving you all lonesome

After all the years we've been through together
Is this tsunami at our age worth for us to weather

Good, bad or ugly we were quite inseparable
Right now, I'd give anything to make us repairable

You can call me weak or utter any profanity you want
But her strength is now my suffering to haunt

Yet, I can't see myself living like a sadfuck
It's like being stuck inside of an old garbage truck

Everything inside feels dead even if it's alive
I'm not sure how to handle all this shit and still survive!

A 40-Year Mindfuck

How can you say "I love you" to me for forty fucking years

But say "I don't love you" and change so fast your gears

For sure you must realize that what you're doing is insane

This pain feels like you're hanging my balls on a big ass crane

You can't just drive your forklift into reverse

Once you've been going forward for better not worse

Maybe you haven't always been the operator

But you can't jump so fast on the damn excavator

The weeds, debris and dead limbs for sure need a cleanup

And perhaps we've let many of them just pile up

There are a lot of beautiful wildflowers let's never forget

That we've cultivated journeying into our sunset

We've kept our garden watered better than most

But without allowing in the sun, the soil loses compost

We are reaping what we've sowed you and I

Despite the dark clouds we have always looked up to the blue sky

But now you want to bring down a torrential rain

To wash away all the good soil and have only a big sinkhole to remain

Together, we have spent much time plowing our seeds of creation

Why waste the rest of our days digging our grave of destruction

Perhaps you like to drive your bulldozer to help you rebuild

I prefer a dump truck to haul the junk and save what's on our fertile field

So are you ready for me to back up this dump truck

Or is the love for me washed out and our marriage is a 40-year mindfuck!

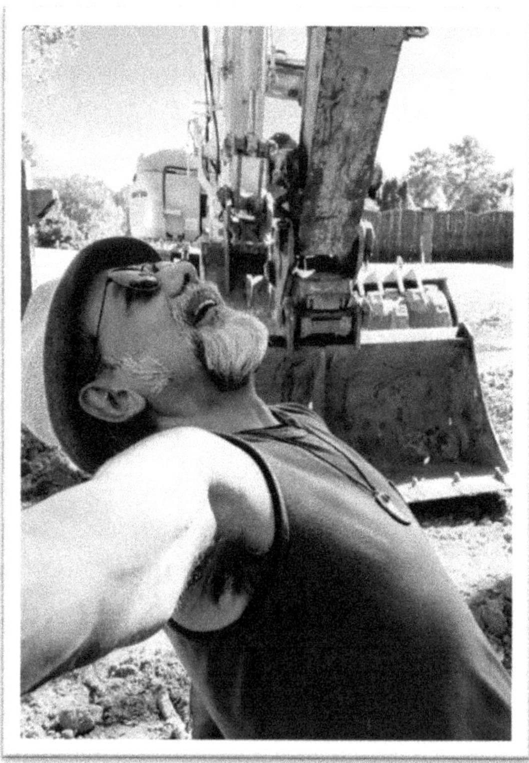

Selfie by Jim Peera

Tell Me Shaman

Tell me Shaman what happened in those sweats
And how you got your mind burning like hot briquettes

Your experiences at a Native Indian sweat lodge
Have got you thinking about our long-lasting love on a dislodge

Inside the steaming hot cylindrical stoned hut
Did you expose your truth or did the ego mislead the gut

Because when you came back you were not the same
Your Spirit was seduced by some unsacred flame

Your eyes pierced me like a dragon in a cage
I've never seen them display such internal rage

Your mouth turned into a heated stone
It was dry, hard and burned me when it was thrown

Your tongue looked like it was freshly dipped in fire
It was hot, angry and the last to retire

Your heart was often cold and it showed little sympathy
I was baffled how it had lost for me much empathy

Your skin that bled toxins out like a waterfall
It did it for your renewal, not your downfall

Your lungs and organs that worked beyond limitation
They did not sign up for your emotional mutilation

Your head with visions of the groundhog that kept churning
Mindfucked you into thinking this love story was worth burning

Your mind, body and soul that you brought to recover
Are trying to make sense of what it is you want to discover

The ancestors and the spirits who appeared in your mind's eye
Don't have the power to lure you into the abyss of the dark sky

They only bring confirmation of what's already in your head
It's always up to you to pick your dance with the living or the dead

So, tell me my Shaman wife, if you're so wise and close to the Divine
What's worth so much to sweat for with actions so asinine

I thought you were a master healer and antidote for those in pain
Not the servant of an angry dark spirit tied to a fiery ball and chain.

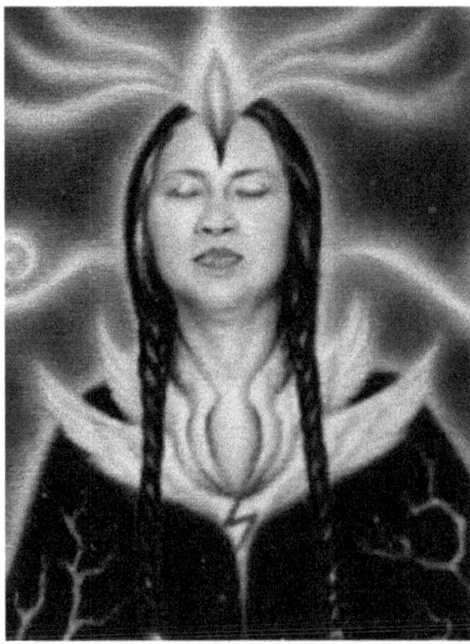

"Shaman Healer" by Toni Taylor

Double Standard

If I just told you I was gay or even bi
Would it matter if I was a gal or a guy

What if a woman always invaded a man's privacy
And caused him much frustration and anxiety

Would she be held to the same standard
As he fights being called a controlling bastard

She can get away making fun of him and saying he's a fat ass
But call her heavy, and you'll pay dearly and be labeled a dumbass

Are we blinded by indifference
And does gender make a difference

Yes, I believe it definitely does
You see gals now get a free pass just because

I'm talking about double standard my friend
Something we must not deny, justify, normalize or defend

Whether you agree with me or not
It starts on the day you tie the marriage knot

The guy's got a gun pointed to his little and big head
While the girl is acting like a princess in bed

Has the imbalance of male patriarchy
Flipped to a woman's newfound hierarchy

Is it the modern world swinging into new order
A western alibi for creating another men's mental disorder

Why is a man always walking on eggshells and on the defense
As his female partner gets away being on the ugly offense

Her acrimony is viewed as a normal life stage
But he's unfairly framed as a chauvinistic outrage

When a woman's liberation is cheered and celebrated
A man's freedom is smeared, feared and castrated

It reminds me of my Muslim brothers in the West Bank
Undeservedly stuck inside of a human fish tank

They're thrown out of spite and apathy into an incarcerated state
With no empathy from those who choose to justify their hate.

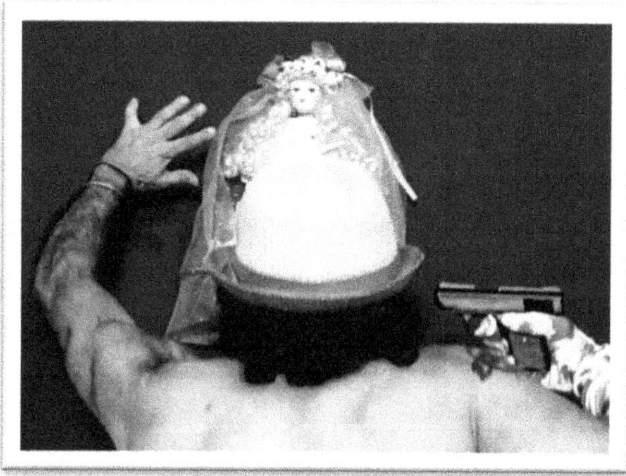

Selfie by Jim Peera

Virginal Itch

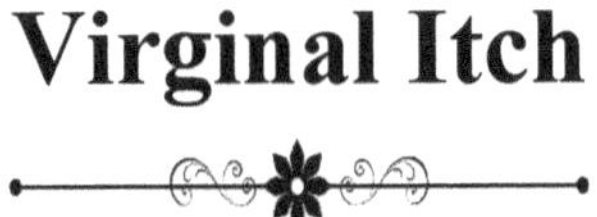

I love hard and have given you everything but a vagina

It's what you now desire and I'm getting a mild case of angina

Perhaps it's just a phase you're going through in life

A price a man pays for choosing a virgin as a wife

You view your new freedom to be fun and easy to handle

I see it as a hand caught in a candy jar, easy to mishandle

Many will dip into your sweet and fiery delights

So, watch out for your wallet when they put out the lights

Whether you fancy the new fruits of a him or a her

I know in the end it will be my banana you'll come to prefer

United we've loved, lived, laughed and cried

Divided we'll slip and tumble into a slippery landslide

So, go ahead my sweet woman and satisfy your virginal itch

Just don't scratch hard or you'll fall into a regrettable wet ditch.

A Tree That Cannot Be Erased

A man's legacy is defined by his work more than his word
Where his temporary journey begins and ends is not in his hands
Yet, when one young man falls in love with a pretty but hurt caged bird
He promises to liberate her and plants the seed for their life plans

This ambitious man diligently waters the plant and helps it grow
He provides love, protection and loyalty for the bird to heal and soar
As the tree flourishes, the healing bird sings and dances aglow
Together, the man and the bird build their nest for a family of four

Forty years pass with many twists, turns, valleys, and mountains
And through it all the bird flies higher than she ever dreamed
The tree they nourished grows branches of abundance like fountains
As this man envisions dying without regrets and a life esteemed

Feeling courageous to reveal her innermost secret to the man
The transformed bird drops a bomb on the love of her life
She reveals that she's gay or bi, one morning in the Yucatan
Mindfucking the sleepy man who is filled with confusion and strife

Then says the head-scratching man to the liberated bird:
My fear is attending each other's funeral as an ex-spouse
Our tree is too beautiful and its roots are firmly grounded to be razed
The empty hole it leaves will serve only the haters as an outhouse
But our legacy cannot be pissed away, if this tree is not erased.

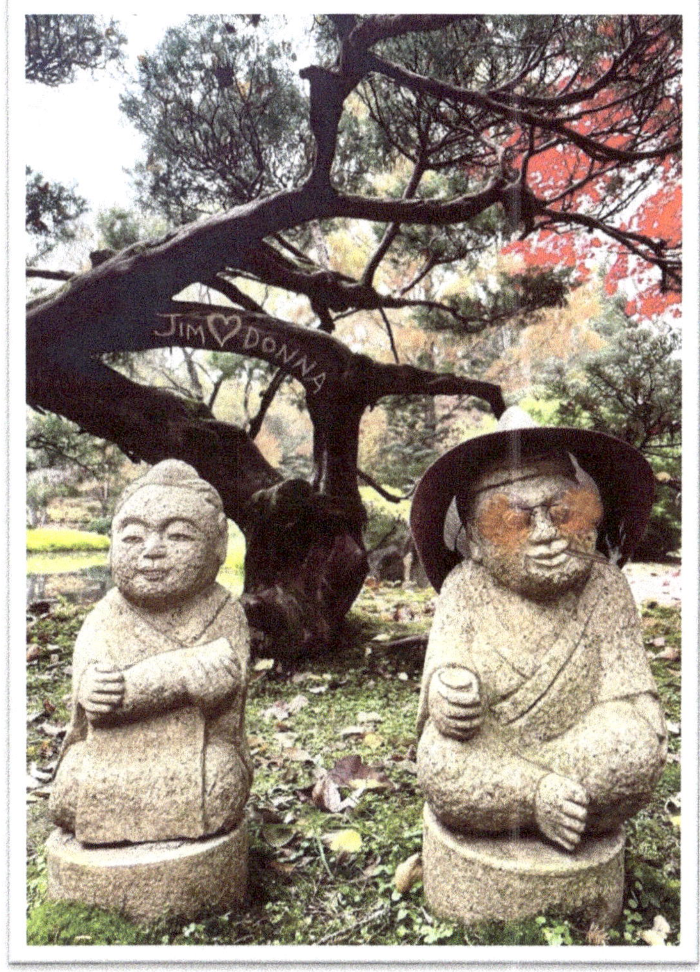

Photo by Jim Peera

"If you love someone, set them free. If they come back, they're yours. If they don't, they never were."

- Richard Bach

The Million Dollar Question

They say every freedom has its price
So don't get excited and think your actions twice

For each ounce of pleasure you'll get
A pound of pain will be yours to fret

A brand new body laying on the white linen bed
Mindfucks you to want to be so comfortably unwed

The full moon excites all your heightened senses
As it strips down and dismantles all your defenses

The secrets your heart has stored for many years
Are now exposed to a gold-digging stranger without fears

Then the morning blue jay incessantly sings
It warns you to beware of your newly liberated wings

Looks like there's an empty space on the cold bed
Now for sure you must feel like a real bonehead

Was it worth it or was it just lust gone absurd
Is then the million-dollar question for this rich free bird.

Punching Bag

I've often been your emotional punching bag
Strong, resilient and soft as a cotton rag

I'm strong, so you dump your weakness on me
Liking me to a grounded oak tree

I'm resilient, so you stretch me as far as I can go
Thinking I'm somewhat made of rubber dough

I'm soft, so you play with me and twist my heart
Knowing I'll always be there and not dart

I'm that outlet you need for relieving your angst and pain
But don't think you can keep pulling my chain

I'm not superhuman or an emotionless robot
Nothing in me is built like a juggernaut

I wasn't born to be kicked around for your fun
From the inside out, I too can be undone

I'm made no different than your own delicate skin
I can tear, puncture and even bleed from within.

But I think I'm an extraordinary punching bag for sure
From the day I was born I learnt to adapt, survive and endure.

Womankind

Sitting on the edge of the railroad track
A teenage girl reflects on her life of strife and lack

I'm gonna die a poor and lonely woman for sure
This life is too sickly and toxic and I see no cure

The house I live in is in a crime infested shit hole
And everything inside slowly sucks my soul

My dad is an unhealed Vietnam vet
My mom says I'm ugly and doesn't keep me fed

Then a fast-moving train abruptly stops in front of the girl's sad eyes
Jump on board and tell me what do you dream and fantasize

I want to be happy and travel around the world for one
And to marry a good man who will be a ball of adventure and fun

The girl takes a risk and steps on the train that has no doors
I'll make your wishes come true, it says, I'm all yours

The train and the beautiful girl go to places many would daydream
Egypt to China to Europe to Latin America and countries in between

She eats the best gourmet cuisine and food money can buy
And sleeps on the best beds without fear or any outcry

The girl feels so safe and protected that she never hops off
Getting on this train has been for her a great payoff

What an amazing journey we're on she says to the train
We can keep going many more years on this fast lane

Then says the girl to the train, I want to get off at the next station
This journey has been great but I need to find my own destination

And where is that, asks the train in a bewildered state
Isn't this the dream journey you were seeking with a soulmate

Yes, but it was your journey that I was riding on all along
And it has made me happy, rich and headstrong

So, for what it's worth I may not be gone for too long
I just want to be my own train and I don't think that's wrong

I know that's really derailing your state of mind
But you showed it to me, Mr. fast train...my womankind!

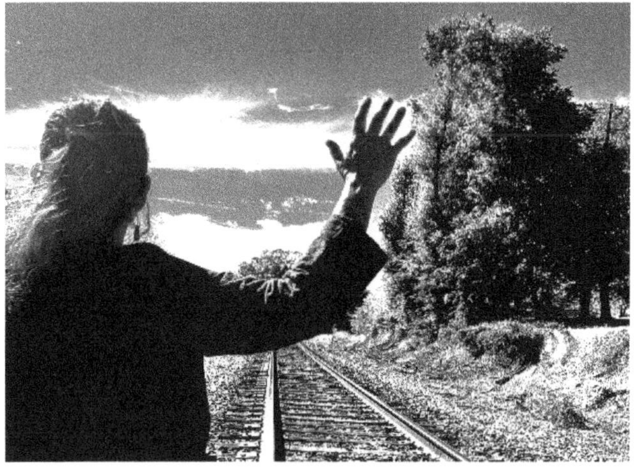

Photo by Jim Peera

I Love You Too Much

Thank you, Bees Gees for one of my favorite tunes y'all wrote
But it's been both a bad karma and a perfect scapegoat

I shoulda known from the start to see the sign
That this relationship may be heading into a landmine

When my young wife heard 'I Love You Too Much' she said in dismay
Why the hell do you love me so much anyway

I guess she didn't love herself back then
Or was it a hidden contempt for men and my own omen

Not sure from what extraterrestrial crystal she's lit
But earthlings here would see her comment as some crazy shit

There's not enough love in the world to go around
We can't take it for granted and drive its goodness to the ground

For sure her power animal the groundhog wants her close to it
I'm perplexed to see her go that far under and submit

Looks like she's letting a random animal take over her life
Or is this a planned-out exit strategy from my wife

Thanks for leaving me and saying you're tired of using me as a crutch
Guess I'm guilty of loving you a little too much

Perhaps I just blasted you with a lot of sun
And it blinded you by firing on me a loaded gun

I thought our relationship was in pretty good balance
Maybe the lesson is for you to be shown a karmic counterbalance

So, rather than fussing and fighting about it all
In the next lifetime, we'll meet again and I'll be your unloving asshole!

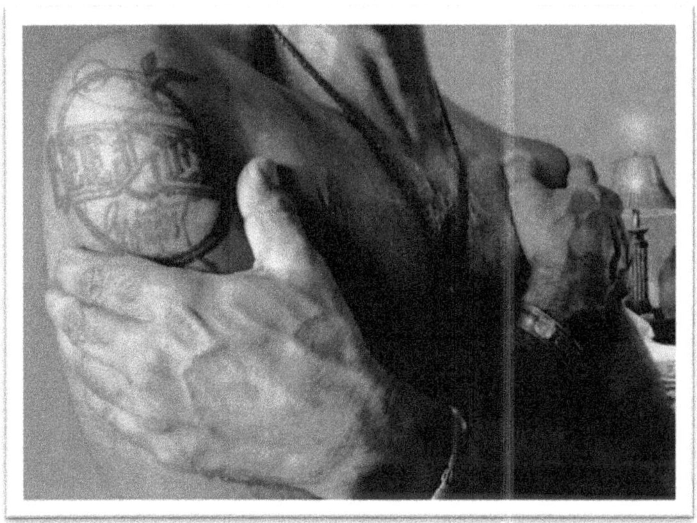

'I Love You Too Much'

A mind-blasting selfie video created as an art installation by Jim Peera
and available <u>exclusively</u> for readers of this book!

YouTube   or   JimPeera.com

Misled

Why are you tossing me into the white vitreous China bowl
That commode is to purge our mind and body in whole

The bathroom mirror reflects on us without a lie
It clearly shows I haven't been an ass or a shitty guy

But I'm having mind constipation, no matter what I do
Lately I'm under-appreciated and not enough for you

Often you told me you loved me when we did whoopee
Now you screw me in the head with a plan to leave me

For so long you'd kiss me like an angelic wife
Today my heart feels cut with a devil's knife

It's not like I haven't spent enough time on you
Yet, you want to flush me out without giving me a clue

You got me tossing and turning into the night
My bowel's churning like it's poisoned by a snakebite

For sure I'm unraveling in a sea of confusion
As my lonely and achy body drowns with self-delusion

I am so ready to unfuck this restless mind's pain
Perhaps a puppet master is pulling my chain

As the morning mirror clears my watery eyes to reveal
I see it's me who's controlling the crappy thoughts I feel

All our attachments, stories and lies trap us from within
It's best to let go and excrete them all for any heal to begin

So, now I've come to realize my brain has just been misled
Because it's you, who's all clogged up with a soiled head!

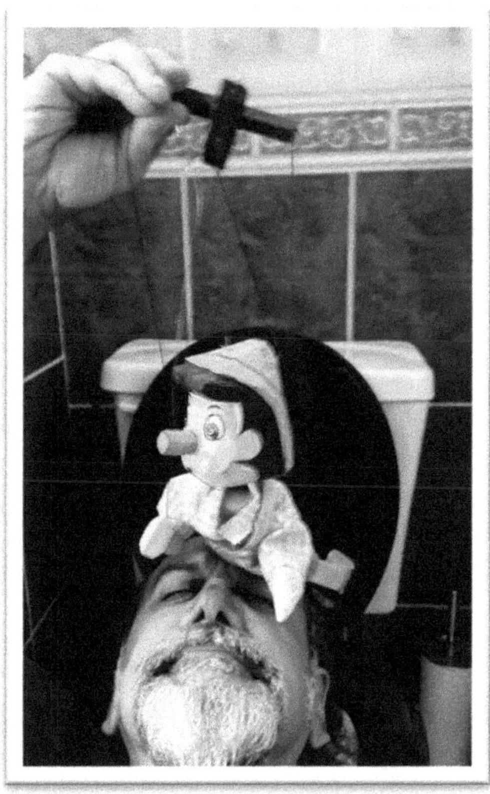

Selfie by Jim Peera

Midas Crutch

I'm the man with the Midas touch, so I'm told
Having a track record of turning everything into gold

If a man's wealth is ultimately measured by his work and deeds
Then you can say that this man surely succeeds

I had a good feeling about a girl and asked her to be my wife
She called me a shining star and together we lit each other's life

I started out lighting my fire with just a handful of shucks
But I got creative and ended up being worth a lot more bucks

A rich and famous fashion designer I did not become
Yet I hustled and sowed many sources of income

The carpet cleaning biz was conventional and boring
So, I took it to unknown heights and saw money pouring

The real-estate market was exciting and worth exploring
I learned to invest, develop, flip and saw my net worth soaring

The art arena was conventional and rather tame
I made it extraordinary and helped thousands of souls reclaim

But now it's all in my rear view as yesterday's story
This accomplished man feels tarnished losing his glory

Everything that has kept me happy and alive seems to be dying
My marriage, vocation and investments are not high flying

This king of hearts is being played by the wild and crazy joker
Has my winning hand turned from great to mediocre

What has happened to me and my Midas touch
And am I being mindfucked into using it as my life's crutch.

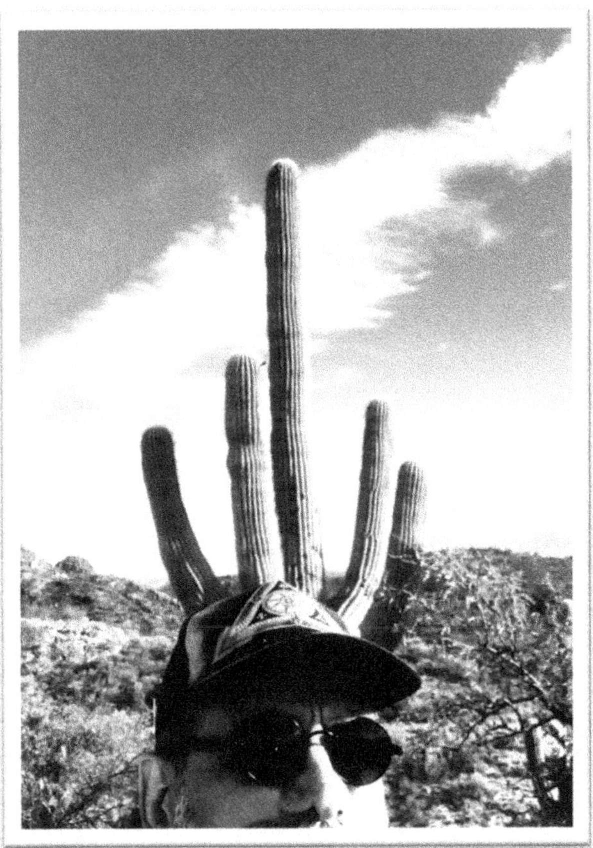

Selfie by Jim Peera

Love Story

This love story of ours was not crafted from fiction
We created it out of our hearts, not out of a duty of dereliction

From the very first page I knew it was going to be a good read
No matter what the heading, each chapter was going to succeed

We kept the reader always intrigued and excited
Because it was all real and we were seldom shortsighted

The ending was never written but it was planned to be a happy one
I remember saying that to you before we even begun

Our roles started out as innocent protagonists
But now we're turning them into guilty antagonists

Somehow the entire book has been changed and given a low rating
Looks like it has vacillated in the process of your selective editing

We can't publish our storybook journey as it sits
Most readers won't buy it, knowing it was never in the pits

You see our life story was written before we were born
You told me so, many times before your present scorn

Both of us are but co-writers of this real-life love of fire
We must not tear out the good pages and turn it into a tragic satire

But no matter how this book is published with your version of the story
I'm at peace to know that my God knows the truth in all his glory.

I've Gotta Get a Message to You

The music of the Bee Gees has been my therapy in my life's trial and tribulations since I can remember. In this particular incident, the Gibb brothers' compositions were even more instrumental in giving me some peace of mind. To show my appreciation, I wrote this poem directed to my wife with many of their songs (shown in CAPS):

Wow, what a MORNING OF MY LIFE! I've been CRYING EVERYDAY since your WORDS pierced me like an ARROW THROUGH THE HEART. You told me you were NOT IN LOVE AT ALL with me and left me all ALONE to deal with the biggest STORM of my life.

TOMORROW, TOMORROW who knows, I may think different. But right IN THE NOW, I'M WEEPING and I'VE GOTTA GET A MESSAGE TO YOU.

Now BABY AS YOU TURN AWAY, why did you have to do this shit to us and be such a HEARTBREAKER?

I've had THE LONGEST NIGHT tormenting inside, how our LOVE SO RIGHT turned for you so wrong? Looks like there was a nasty CHAIN REACTION after your mom died and we've been busy losing our SACRED TRUST for each other. Ever since then, you've just been BLOWING A FUSE!

There's a lot of EMOTION running through me right now. I CAN'T HELP IT feeling GUILTY about things that I could have done better to keep this relationship STAYING ALIVE, living our not so ORDINARY LIVES.

And we've led an extraordinary life YOU AND I. If you leave me, this will be a real TRAGEDY. There's TOO MUCH HEAVEN in our marriage for it to be EATEN ALIVE.

Since YOU STEPPED INTO MY LIFE, I've been CRAZY FOR YOUR LOVE and even now I COULD NOT LOVE YOU MORE. So, you can never tell anyone REALLY AND SINCERELY that this husband of mine, well HE'S A LIAR about having loved me.

Not sure why you can just stop TO LOVE SOMEBODY who's been CLOSER THAN CLOSE to you than anyone in your whole life. I'm trying to SEARCH, FIND but may never unearth the truth behind HOW DEEP IS YOUR LOVE for me at this time.

You say I LOVE YOU TOO MUCH and you don't understand why. But WHAT KIND OF FOOL thinks that way? As long as we've been LIVING TOGETHER, you never stopped saying YOU LOVE ME and I've helped bring out the best of THE WOMAN IN YOU.

So, what kind of JIVE TALKING are you giving me now MY EVENING STAR? Do I need EYES THAT SEE IN THE DARK to make sense of your sudden WIND OF CHANGE? Or are you teaching me a LESSON IN LOVE?

You say you have no SECRET LOVE in your life. And that I am only GUILTY of committing a CRIME OF PASSION and being a MAN ON FIRE. Yes, for sure on many occasions, I've even given you much SENSUALITY and a NIGHT FEVER!

That's because my DESIRE for you was always real in this earthly KISS OF LIFE. You were a WOMAN IN LOVE and we have been THE ONLY LOVE for each other. DON'T FORGET TO REMEMBER this truth.

Maybe I gave you TOO MUCH HEAVEN and a taste of PARADISE too soon to appreciate me. I know without doubt that I kept many of my PROMISES to make you happy, flutter like a BUTTERFLY and be MORE THAN A WOMAN.

Everyone saw our WORLD as a marriage of AN EVERLASTING LOVE. Never were we about SMOKE AND MIRRORS. I even wrote how our LOVE IS THICKER THAN WATER in my book where I made you SHINE SHINE from start to finish!

There will be LONELY DAYS ahead of me IF I CAN'T HAVE YOU. Not sure HOW CAN YOU MEND A BROKEN HEART after four decades. I guess I'LL KISS YOUR MEMORY and be SHADOW DANCING to get me some PEACE OF MIND for myself.

Our love for each other is SHATTERPROOF and goes ABOVE AND BEYOND. So DON'T THROW IT ALL AWAY, my dear. We must try our best to keep it ALIVE and complete our destined LIFE STORY.

I CAN'T HELP IT to now SURRENDER to my God who hears MY LOVER'S PRAYER at this time. This IRRESISTABLE FORCE is not of the UNDERWORLD and knows that this EXPERIENCE I'm going through cannot be THE END OF THE RAINBOW for us.

In the end, our LOVE NEVER DIES and I WANNA GO HOME WITH YOU when we're called up to see our GOD'S GOOD GRACE. So, STOP THINK AGAIN, and PLEASE DON'T TURN OUT THE LIGHTS.

This is ONE LOVE that's definitely deserving of IMMORTALITY... and we don't say goodbye!

Power of Truth

I've spent my whole life building my man power
So don't think I'll let any woman allow it to cower

My heart is soft and radiates with goodness
Don't take it as a sign of my weakness

My brain is not connected below my waist
Any attempt to twist it will be in haste

The playbook of projection is your mind's trick
It reveals all your covered flaws, says the shrink

A mother hen is not going to pull my emotional chain
This soul has come too far to be flushed down any drain

A woman's liberation is not a healthy movement
Unless it's first about working on her own self-improvement

Your beauty may get men to lose their heads and rollover
But this one ain't no pansy that you can pushover

So, before you fuss and point to all the faults in me
Look into your own mirror and I bet you will see

There's just no damn way you can disempower me
Because it's you that must set your own truth free.

Light of My Life

Starlight why do you fuck with me
And show yourself as a bright light that would be

I look up to you in the dark sky
But you are not there as you're just an illusive lie

You shine from millions of light years away
Only to blind me into thinking you'll always stay

You fool me into pleasing me with your radiant charm
Not knowing that your seduction does me great harm

My lonely days that you've made so bright
Were they real or blindly distorted in my hindsight

You were there but you really were not there
Because if you were, my heart would be in less of a tear

I know your light left long ago, for me to now clearly see
But why did you pretend all along to be joyful, happy and so free

For many years my eyes were aligned in your universe of delight
Wish I knew you were planning one day to drop me out of your sight

They say our present reality is a reflection of the past
And to make the most of it, as it does not last

So starlight, stop screwing with my head and playing with my life
You are but a spotlight in the past... not dissimilar to my wife.

Life Goes Fast

The saying 'time flies when you're having fun' has been a reality for me
I'm sure you my dear would not also disagree

Our life together has gone fast as we've had much adventure and fun
We've rode it above and beyond the clouds and kissed the sun

The car we drove through the valleys and mountains was sporty
It zipped, zagged and got us out of ditches from zero to forty

The plane we piloted was akin to an unmanned rocket ship
It wasn't afraid to step on the pedal to give us a great trip

The ship we sailed on was much more than a speedboat
It cut through the biggest waves and always kept us afloat

The bus we drove was an open double-decker in design
It served us well and gave us the best views of every skyline

The train we manned on our track had no marked destination
It never forgot to stop and pick up anyone at every station

The fluttering wings of a white Pegasus you saw in your vision of me
Is the truth of our epic ride together, most couples never foresee

Now every moment we don't spend as one is like walking on one foot
It requires each of us to have a crutch as a substitute

So why put the brakes on us now my dear and slow our beautiful life down
It may just turn us into two sadfucks eager to count every sundown.

Walk of Life

Our walk in the park is not quite the same for you and me
Yours is with sneakers and mine is bare feet and carefree

The path you like to walk on is often paved, smooth and hard
Mine is alongside yours but it's akin to a softer and uneven backyard

You like to walk briskly and make many rounds
I prefer to take my time and cover all the park grounds

Your feet are tightly covered and cushioned to protect you
Mine are bare and vulnerable to walk into any type of doo doo

You carry your phone to keep yourself with others connected
I like it on mute to enjoy my break and be happily disconnected

You got leaves and sticks that may blow onto your concrete footpath
I got weeds, rocks and bare soil that give me a nature footbath

The raw area I walk on is a reminder for me to stay real and grounded
It beats being on the hot surface with people all fake and bounded

In all our differences though, we've always kept walking aside in unity
So why run away from making positive strides until perpetuity

The path we choose to walk on is up to each of us you see
No matter where it leads, the journey has to feel alive and free

Many birds and butterflies fly around to give us humans a clue
To touch and feel the green grass and look up to the sky so blue

The sun shines on the park no matter what walking path we take
It radiates better on us when our feet are exposed and wide awake

So, the next steps we'll take in life will determine where we go
Walk on our lighted path together, or be lost in each other's shadow.

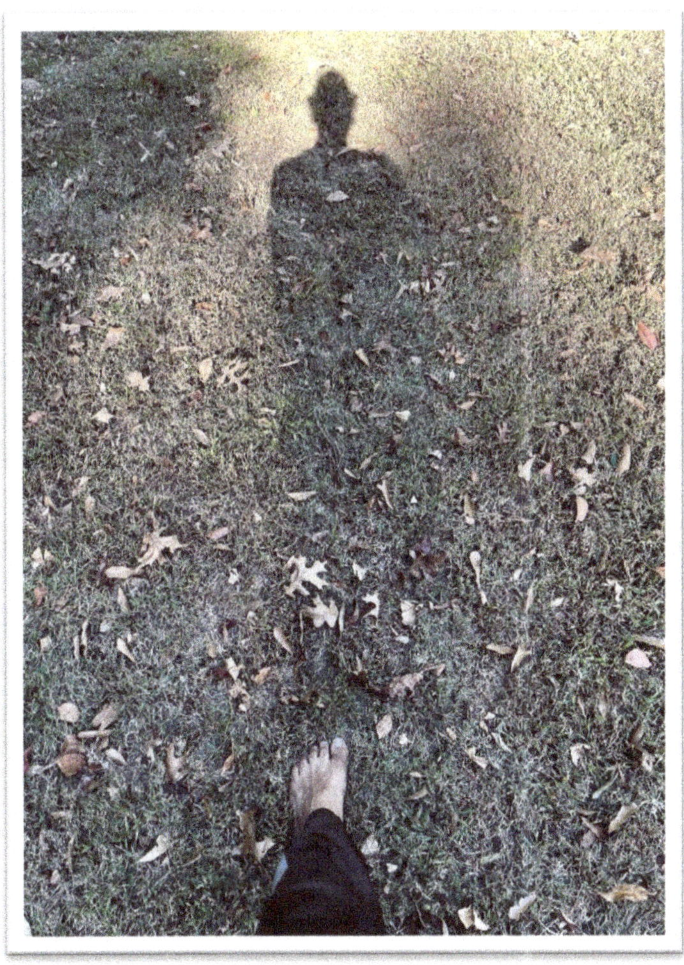

Selfie by Jim Peera

Space

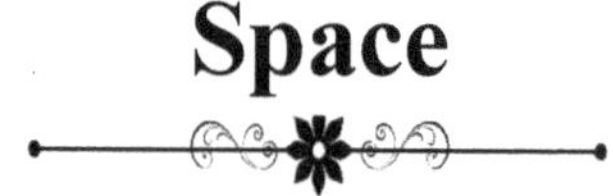

If space is your next and final Spiritual frontier my dear
It's surely instilling in me some degree of head-scratching fear

Time away is great, but there's a risk in your desire to be alone
Exploring your inner void can get you lost in the unknown

You believe you're entering a stage of self-discovery renaissance
And life would be wasted without taking your last chance

But only fate will show itself through the cosmic tea leaves
As it knows how often the mind plays tricks and deceives

The stories it tells to trap and misguide the inner voice
Can seduce even the smartest ones to make a wrong choice

How many past beautiful memories can be simply erased
While the bad ones will be magnified and seamlessly interlaced

It is in the emptiness of our distance that darkness fills
The onus then, is on each of us to not light up our past ills

So, I hope in the earthly space that we are now apart
We won't disengage from the universal truth in each other's heart.

You Will Be Back

You will be back because you love the yin yang in me
It's not just what I did, but what I also didn't do you see

You will be back because I made you laugh more than cry
It's not just to make you happy, but not make you want to die

You will be back because we did more things together
It's loving each other's company in good, but also bad weather

You will be back because we were soulmates as one
It's not just about our purpose and struggle, but all the play and fun

You will be back because we were truly deep in love
It's not just saying *I love you,* but not putting personal hate above

You will be back because we were a power couple you know
It's not just that we made a difference, but we radiated a certain glow

You will be back because we lit up the sky they say
It's not because we made it brighter, but didn't try to dim others day

You will be back because we will be memorialized side by side
It's not that you and I mattered, but our God didn't see our divide

You will be back because in my mind you've always been here
And this is the longest April Fool's joke you've played yet my dear!

Care-Less

My whole life I've been caring and self-less
But now you're teaching me to be selfish and care-less

Your advice is quite a mindfuck for a person like me
To flip and reset my past and present reality

You say why drain yourself for the acceptance of another
You must first fill your own fountain, my life partner

It's important to stay powerful for our own well being
Putting ourselves in first position is not a bad thing

When you're looking out for no one but yourself
You will value and appreciate you, in and of itself

You can't give out what you don't have, they say
Being happy and loving thyself must be our default pathway

Perhaps it's time I start prioritizing myself and to self-care
Or else my life will be lived for others and lead to nowhere

For nothing makes sense and everything makes sense you see
It's the duality of being in balance and setting myself truly free.

So, honey, this advice is like the one you gave me on stimulation
Where you told me to go unfuck myself, using masturbation!

The Total Package

A wiseman knows not to buy into the prettiest package
It's often a coverup hiding a lot of ugly baggage

Its bright and colorful exterior skin is quite thin
Don't prick it as it easily bleeds from within

Its casing looks quite sturdy and strong
Don't damage it, as it has already been so, all along

Its smell is intoxicating and sweet
Don't get lost in it, as it has bitterness to secrete

Its allure is tempting enough to want to open it
Don't rush in yet, as it holds secrets and other deep shit

Its inside comes with an 'as is' no extended warranty
Don't worry, figuring it out will kill you first, I guarantee

These pretty packages come in all shapes, sizes and finds
And they've confounded even the sharpest minds

But I'd rather have a smart and pretty one, than a dumb and ugly one
Why get mindfucked by mediocrity and not have good loving fun

So even after having lived with all of her baggage
I'm grateful to have been gifted someone who has the total package!

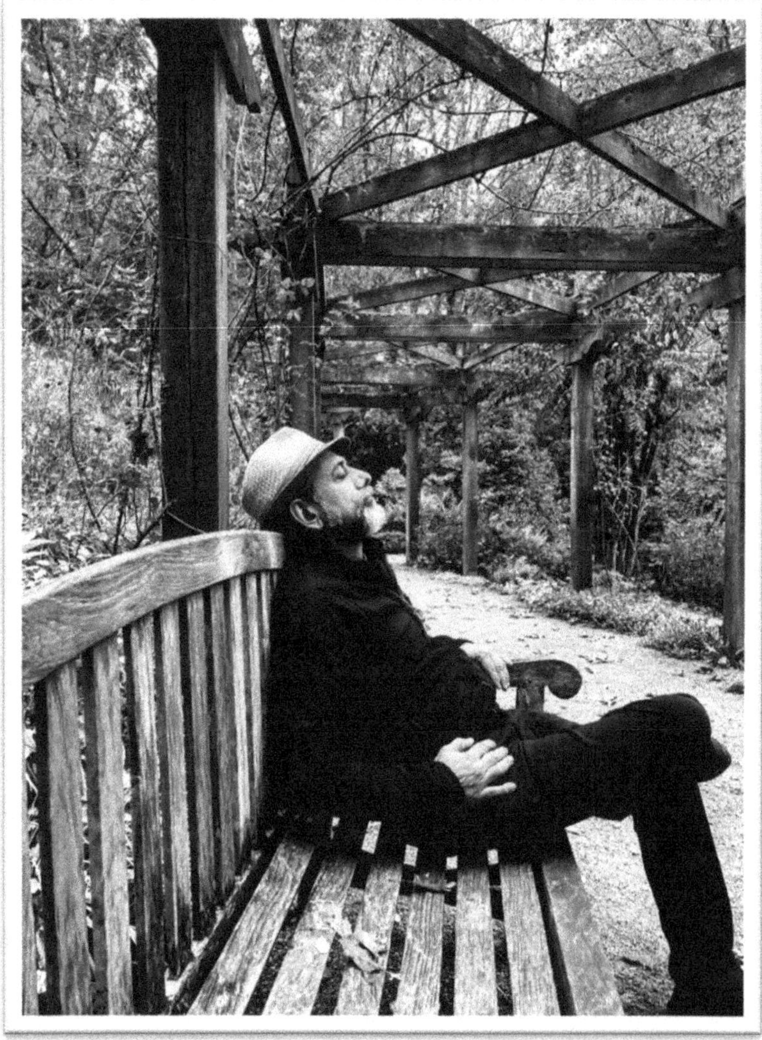

"Alone Naturally"

Selfie by Jim Peera

Alone Naturally

We enter and leave this temporary world alone
There will only be one name written on our tombstone

Aloneness is where true love with thyself begins
It's where all our battles and losses turn into wins

The mind empties, the body repairs its limbs and the soul fills
There's a Divine connection that brings the spine its chills

No one else matters to serve our needs from the outside
Everything we ever needed has always come from the inside

The enlightened ones show us the power of blissfulness
Within each of us lies a life of self-mastery and consciousness

The journey inward is not without fear or trepidation
It has been seduced and manipulated by outwardly validation

But I'm beginning to understand the value of being solitary
As the chains of codependency are cut and ready to bury

Just like a broken bird's nest in the wild after an attack
Your abandonment is showing me much strength to adapt

So, although I may be fine living in this habitat alone naturally
I prefer on us rebuilding and never breaking the unity in our family.

A Rare Gem

God has gifted her with everything, said my mom
You could have never found such a girl in Dar es salaam

She's like an uncut yellow diamond, but full of white light
Even more beautiful and precious than a purple blue Tanzanite

Your dad would have been proud of this Bella Donna
But before you marry her, we must rename her Farhana

Her name means happy and yours means protector and great
Together you will surely manifest your Divine fate

This shy and innocent virgin never felt so loved
Being with a man who promised she wouldn't ever be unloved

Their wedding sucked and the honeymoon was a cheap joke
But their marriage grew stronger akin to a roots of a big red oak

Despite their disparate culture, upbringing and color
None were able to tarnish this couple and turn them any duller

Both were created with a wealth of talent and to amaze
She, endowed with metaphysical gifts and he, born to trailblaze

Together they've showered the world with love worthy of their destiny
Healing so many and even unearthing the unhealed with jealousy

Being unconventional and real, they're often misunderstood
Similar to an artist who brings life to a piece of dead driftwood

Four decades have flown with much adventure, joy and pleasure
As Azim and Farhana have made their mark many would treasure

The couple's crystal mothership is eagerly waiting for their arrival
Until then, they must stay alight and endure their earthly survival

You're such a shining couple, said a Healium attendee to one of them
Thanks, replied Azim, our love story is none other than a rare gem!

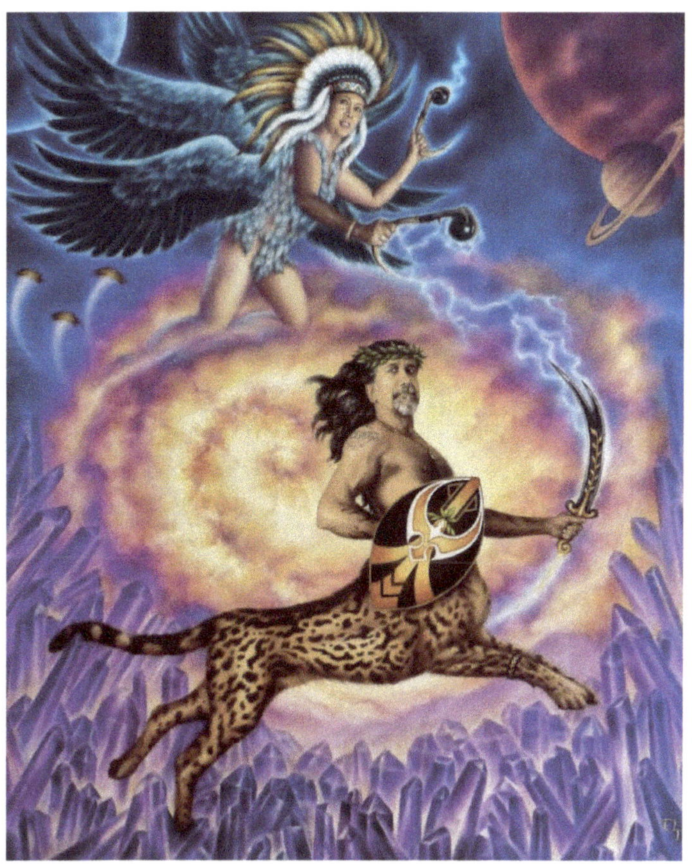

Artist: Toni Taylor

In The Shadow of a Shaman

A shaman knows how the forest echoes the voices of the foolish and the wise
With this truth every tree knows nature's duality before it dies

From the morning sun that kisses on its treetop
To the evening shadow that reflects an oncoming teardrop

Every tree gathers all memories within itself, from good to bad
And knows what to keep if it wants to grow into a mighty granddad

The roots have seen and heard everything walking on their path
From a happy dog that relieves itself to a sick and sad psychopath

Nothing is guaranteed, as it knows it reaps what it sows
It lives one day at a time until it confronts the roaring backhoes

The screaming sounds it hears of the machine deafens its senses
But it has nothing planned to fight in its arsenal of defenses

The flawed leaders have gathered and acted as judge, jury and executioner
Now at best, the tree's fate is to be a piece of art for some lonely gardener

Yet, the sun will shine and the rain will puddle in its emptied hole
As another seed fills and grows again to become alive and whole

Perhaps this time the tree will be more beautiful than ever before
Attracting the lovers, not the haters under this much wiser sycamore

Its hugging canopy will provide much shade for everyone underneath it
And no one will find a need to harm it or even ask for a removal permit

So why should I be lost in the shadow of my woman Shaman now
When I need to be wiser, grounded and defend the truth in my own powwow!

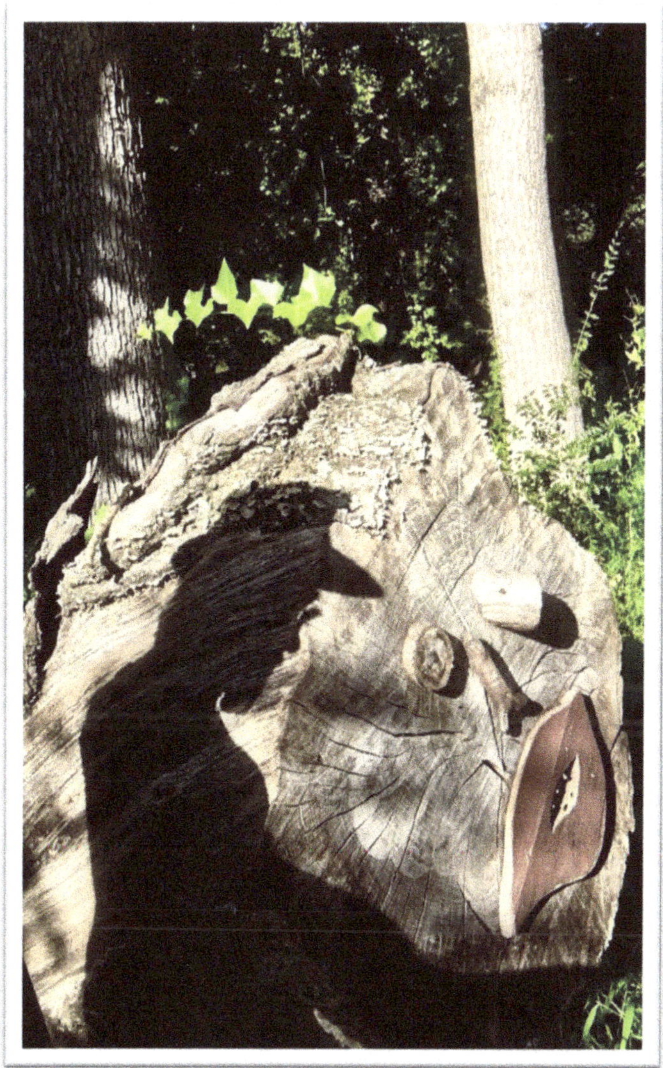

Selfie by Jim Peera

In The Now

The sunbeam on my face cracks open the eyes to wake up
It reminds the unrested brain to stop thinking of my recent breakup

I'm tired but I'm fixated at the sight and sounds of the bright outdoors
It's more alive and joyful than what's presently for me indoors

Then two love birds crash in the middle of a large window pane
They sing aloud and dance as if to entertain

There's a sound of a familiar baby hawk not too far from me
It knows it's safe and protected perched atop the highest canopy

As a powerful wind rustles through an oak tree, a squirrel jumps on it
It runs up a branch, slips down, gets up, and just won't quit

Through another window pane, a huge spider web has formed
In a very short time, it has built itself strong and transformed

What a powerful lesson these creatures are teaching me today
Who don't seem to dwell on any bad shit from yesterday

Everything in this idyllic moment seems to want to stand still
It's a new day and these few minutes have opened my soul to refill

I say 'I am powerful, I am protected, I am prosperous, I am peace'
It's my morning mantra to ground myself and not let my Spirit cease

As I get out of bed and make my way to the bathroom
A mirror on the left holds my attention to wisely illume

A reflection of a well-aged naked body holds my balding head
Inside of it sits a mysterious enemy that often acts as a warhead

It loves to tease and seduce me with fun memories of the past
Until an angelic voice outside cleverly interrupts to counterblast

Be glad you're alive this morning you foolish overthinking man
Stay in the now and empty your brain of any future grand plan!

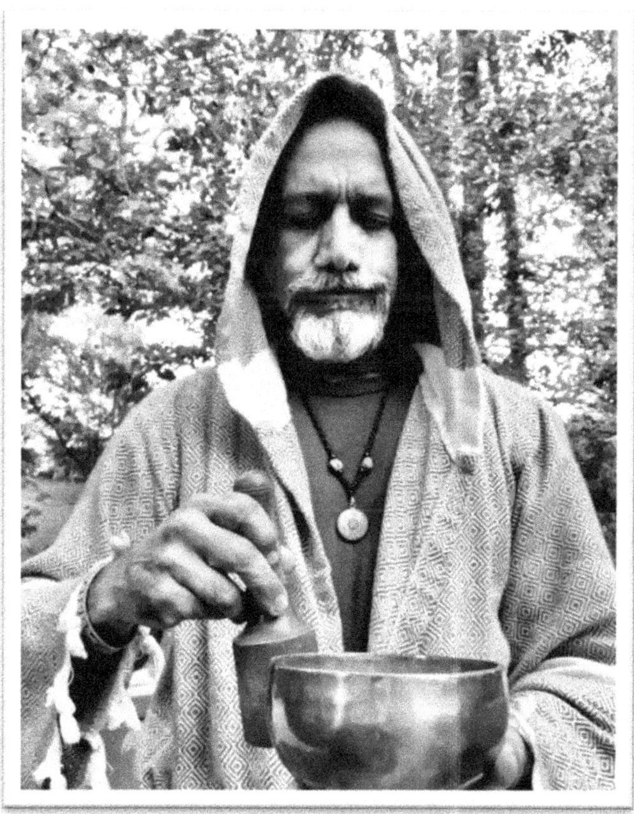

Selfie by Jim Peera

The Solutions Guy

Bitch to me about all your problems, but I'm a solutions guy

My end game is to go beyond the who, the what and the why

I got but one life here and I can't see it fucking mine or yours

So being creative is my answer to fixing all our internal wars

Your symptoms are your friend, not to hideaway or to bury

They point to some hidden shit, making your ethos unsanitary

The pain you're feeling in your heart is weakness leaving the body

Don't numb it as the suffering is building in you a strong antibody

The emotions that are consuming you like waterfalls

Don't try to stop them if you want to break down your walls

The depression you're under is debilitating you, I can see

Don't feed that fear beast, it will starve you from being free

The temperature change inside you is rising rapidly up

Don't be too slow to cool it down, or you'll just blowup

The stress you're battling within is revealing your imbalance

Don't you know the Western world knows little balance

Is all the damage you're doing to yourself worth the price

For sure it's not buying you a ticket to any earthly paradise

So how about you bring me your blocked and rusty parts

And I'll jolt them to restart our broken hearts

We need to open them back and get our high energy flowing

It's what we've always done by keeping our inner lights glowing

You know I am a creative solutions guy you can always come to

Together, we can turn any damn breakdown into a breakthrough!

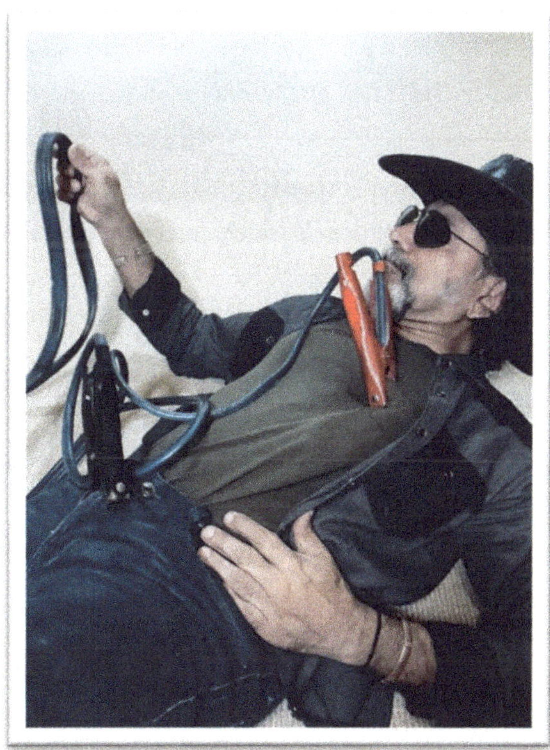

Selfie by Jim Peera

I n 2006 I had nasal surgery for polyps where the doctor went too deep and damaged some olfactory nerves. "Oh shit!" I said, not knowing I couldn't even smell that. Having lost most of my smell, my life has not been the same ever since. During the breakup period, it became even more pronounced and I was inspired to write this poem while I was daydreaming of my wife as I was relaxing in the forest:

Escential

Knock, knock, who's trying to come in my barn door
Is it you Jim, who can't smell shit anymore?

Yep, and it's not fun losing my sense of smell
My life feels half empty and I want to enjoy it well

Almost everything seems mute, tasteless and lame
Wonder how long my passion and libido will still remain

The flowers, the food and the fresh air have lost their glory
They've been amputated from my normal sensory

A morning cup of espresso has no distinct aroma
It's as if my nose has gone into a long ass coma

The cigar I smoke is just an expensive pacifier
I might as well be inhaling a fancy stick of fire

All I taste is bitter and sweet in a gin and tonic
Someone please tell me this condition is not chronic

Like a ray of sunshine breaking through the forest so dense
Perhaps a day comes soon to awaken my lost sense

For my nose has died, but my eyes have never been so alive
And for sure, both are necessary for a good sex drive

So, honey can you call the playful fairies and nature Spirits now
To shine some light on this man afraid of losing his mojo somehow

I'm in the woods dreaming of smelling and entering you once more
It's escential, I not lose my way through your front and back door!

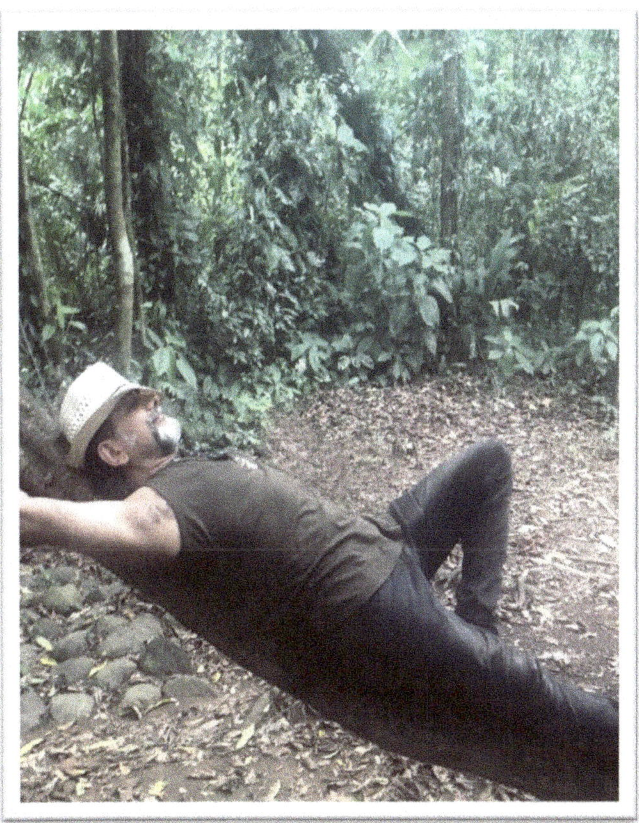

Selfie by Jim Peera

Divine Gift

He wakes me up in the middle of the night
His energy so strong it's hard for a man to fight

He's there when I'm lonely and during all my trials
This almighty creation is revered by both Jews and gentiles

He's seen by many as a savior for their purpose and being
For sure he has risen on many occasions for our wellbeing

He's the most complex phenomenon known to man
Even science knows little how his power really began

He's so connected to me from the inside out
That no matter how I doubt, I cannot do without

He's that love-hate relationship every human carries
Many women have even become his adversaries

He's definitely not a one-size fits all creation
Big or small, his believers always get a good sensation

He's good at playing with my big head though
In pain it wants a blow, and in pleasure it likes to grow

He's my Divine partner in crime and no one can fuck with us
You guessed it, he's my incredible extraordinary penis!

Sexy Dancer

They tell me I'm a sexy dancer on the dance floor
And to be careful not to get my body too close to a whore

Thanks, I say but I've already been twerked by many
From old fat asses to young tight ones in their twenty

I can't help it, the rhythm of the beat intoxicates me
It's a healing drug for my Spirit to feel alive and be set free

There's nothing more satisfying than letting myself loose
I'm just there to have clean fun, not seeking to fuck or seduce

The therapy freestyle dancing provides is immeasurable
Plus, it's a great body workout that's highly pleasurable

Dancing keeps me young as I strut around all the pretty women
But I often end up attracting the drunk and sleezy old men

They admire me as they say I'm a renaissance man
A person who lives life to the fullest as much as he can

For some reason they love my dirty dancing moves
I guess my energy is unfiltered, liberating and exciting as it grooves

Whether you're somebody's lonely partner or a bored wife
Jim, the dancing man shows you the meaning of just kissing life

But what nobody warned this sexy old dancer was this;
How a trans hooker would mouthfuck me with a yucky French kiss!

Thank You Honey

Being alive is about always staying grateful
Yet we die inside because we forget being thankful

Gratitude and thankfulness must coexist together
For a love relationship to last in any inclement weather

A healthy marriage is giving a hundred percent for each
This truth is for me much more than a figure of speech

The heavy risks I've taken to bring home the big money
Perhaps you took them all for granted, honey

Were all the little things I've done for you
Not appreciated in the moment and slipped through

Did the mountains I climbed to make you a good living
Just landslide us down by my insatiable giving

Have the valleys I've gotten you in and out of
Got me stuck in an empty dark hole without you to love

I'm not sure if the game you're playing in our life's last inning
Becomes our destined end, or a win-win beginning

But I must thank you for inserting in my heart your hook
As it has lifted me up, by writing this healing poetry book!

During the WTF moment to my breakthrough period that lasted two months, I met many folks at nightclubs, restaurants and bars with stories of bad divorces, unhealthy lifestyles, and loss of personal power. Their journeys inspired me to write some poems that I believe many people can relate to. I offer them here for YOU to get enlightened and unfucked!

This first poem is about a female who interpreted my 'untitled' piece of art that had to do with befriending our shadow. But surrealism art is highly subjective and draws out the truth from our own life experiences. This woman related the piece to herself as a 'maneater.' who sucks a man's power from his penis. Wow, that's an honest and wild interpretation, I thought to myself! And it inspired me to write about it:

Maneater

The woman is wild and secretly admits she's a maneater

What she doesn't reveal is that she's also a man hater

Her hunting ground is full of fat pigs and horny monkeys

It's taught her to seduce more than the usual flunkies and junkies

Why waste your time on the struggling and the unhealed

It's much satisfying screwing with the heads of the more healed

She knows how to lure each one of them into her den of devour

It's her convoluted way of regaining her lost woman power

The bad memories of the past have been brought to center stage

There's some unfinished story that taints her with internal rage

Was it someone in her family or some douche bag in her early life
The damage done has her incapable of being a stable wife

She thinks she's calculated and smart as a whip being a succubus
It's quite a dumb way of getting even with the wrath of an incubus

This woman has been tormented with her story of strife
Watch out man, she'll slice any man's heart with the sharpest knife

Hold on to both your heads too, as they'll get lost in her sweet sucking
She'll spit you out and hang you dry before she even starts fucking

Don't even think you can open her Pandora's Box to discuss
She's trapped and enslaved herself in a cage that's too superfluous

Now, you best stay out of her way and save yourself
Or you'll end up inside of an urn and be another trinket on her shelf

So, thank you maneater for revealing your ravaged soul to me
But you ain't emptying mine, to fill yours and to set it free.

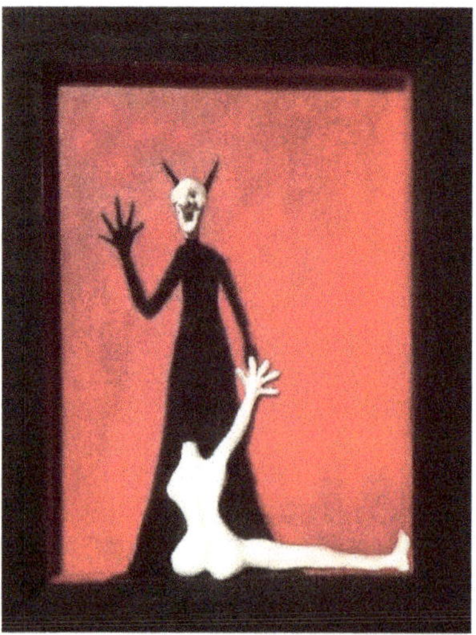

Mixed media art by Jim Peera

Mirror, Mirror

Mirror, mirror on the wall
Who's the most imbalanced sadfuck of them all

Perhaps you're asking me to look at myself without blinders
For sure my friends aren't helping, being softies and enablers

I see my mind is restless and anxious as it thinks too much
So, I fill it with all kinds of drugs as a crutch

This mind is also too fragile and weak as it does not think
I donated it to computers and social media, says the shrink

My body is out of shape, unhealthy and is oversized
I call it body positivity, so it's less ugly and emphasized

This body is also a temple that's trashed with poisoned food
But I like eating my feelings, so please don't intrude

My soul is vacating and held hostage from deep within
There's nothing good to fill it with, so why break in

This soul is also controlled by the mind and the body you see
Until I get both in better shape, it will never be totally free

So mirror, mirror on the wall thanks for playing hardball
Now I must get unfucked and rebalance my mind, body and soul.

Shitshow

Like a laser beam of truth on life's big stage
A man comes to shine some light on a lonely tiger in a cage

As he tries to expose and cancel the darkness from its eyes
It resists by being set in its ways and survives disguised in lies

What the man sees clearly is the tiger's mojo slowly dying
A true reflection of its self-sabotage and a habit of denying

Once upon a time it was passionate, playful and wild
Now it acts like a domesticated animal that's sad and exiled

The man tells it not to justify and normalize this to any degree
Because life's too short and 'if it is to be, it is up to me'

There are a lot more acts to play, so wake up and breakout
Once you open your eyes, you'll see clearly without a doubt

The tiger squints at the man through the bright spotlight
You're blinding me, it says and that causes me to be affright

Being happy is hard to handle and very discomforting
When you befriend and feed your emotional suffering

Please go now so I can retreat in my dark and safe cage
I prefer to be mad, bitter and preoccupied with my internal rage

You may not like that I am choosing to simply resign
This stage is just not my style in its current design

But don't fret, for I am the smartest sadfuck tiger of them all
Quitting this shitshow of life before my final curtain call.

Laissez Faire American

I'm a proud almighty laissez faire American
Don't criticize me or I'll have to draw out my weapon

I have a right to do whatever I damn please
Fuck with me and I'll bring you down to your knees

I was raised without getting a spanking
And in school I always managed to get a high ranking

I ain't that clever and am definitely overrated
But thanks to smartphones I'm not so dumb and hated

I like staying depressed and sick in the head
It gets me all the drugs while I'm a walking dead

I am angry and I hate everyone who is not like me
It sure trumps being happy, kind and carefree

I have very little coping or social skills
Not to worry, I have faith in my prescription pills

I don't like to read, write or dialogue with anyone
This ass is glued to the screen and it's my idea of fun

I am fragile, fickle and always offended
It's just me being 'woke' and emotionally bounded

I am obsessed with myself and love to take selfies
It validates me being a trans and an online striptease

I got skeletons in the closet and traumas unhealed
I prefer to keep them all buried and concealed

I am always anxious with an attention span of a goldfish
Keep entertaining me, it helps me stay selfish

I'm not interested in doing the work to keep anything intact
It's my disposable society's answer to not face any true fact

I love to eat shit and drive my fat ass everywhere
Say what you want but I am proud of this gross derriere

I am a master of complaints and a servant to my ego beast
Go ahead and emulate me, for I am in balance the least

I am really quick to point fingers at everyone but myself
Even my truth mirror looks great collecting dust on the shelf

So yes, I am this badass laissez faire American y'all
I'll do what I damn please, so keep enabling my downfall!

Monogamey

From dusk to dawn they're both dying from within
He stays alive by overworking and she drowns herself in gin

The life they've seemingly built together for so many years
Has got them sinking in a sea of regret and a boatload of fears

He walks around with his head hanging like a weeping willow
She runs around town flirting with anyone who'll lay by her pillow

One look into each other's eyes and you know they've gone stale
The flame is slowly extinguishing inside their self-induced jail

Their most exciting night out is going to a restaurant to eat
It's where their eyes wander on sexy strangers in discreet

They'll mock, ridicule and judge those they most admire
Don't mind, they're just projecting their overdue desire

As the fleeting sun drops off the horizon in a blink of an eye
The man and the woman waste another day waving a sad goodbye

Each will lay side by side tonight like they've done for so long
Both will say they're too tired to fuck and pretend to play along

The full moon looks upon each of them with a crazy gaze
These are the true lunatics who are down there, it says

For sure both of them are good at being poker faced
Wishing their partner for just one starry night could be replaced

Neither has the spine or balls to talk about swinging with some other
They've been programmed by culture and rules to eat no further

That's too bad because even a threesome could reignite their fire
A harmless physical adventure to not feel like a worn-out tire

But the man sneaks out of bed and feasts on an online playmate
As she reaches into her bag of plastic pleasures to masturbate

Yes, they're the sadfuck married couple who play a game of lies
Buying into monogamy and not activating what they fantasize.

Parasite

It's the hungry beast that comes uninvited into your brain
You love it and feed it as it makes you feel special like cocaine

Like an adrenaline rush from performing in front of a huge crowd
It makes you feel validated, special and proud

Similar to the 'Like' button on social media sites
It has the instant ability to catapult you to new personal heights

No different than a powerful shot of steroid up your ass
It gives you an incredible feeling of being a motherfucking badass

In fact, this thing brings you a sense of being invincible
As it makes you believe that all your wins are irreversible

You're immersed so deep in it that it changes your personality
And turns you into a serious sadfuck with a narcissist's mentality

Often you believe that you've 'arrived' as a Spiritual being
Not realizing you're just being deceived and are unseeing

As you walk around with an elevated opinion of yourself
The external high is the pretentious low point of the inner self

Because your arrogance and delusion have blinded you
Deviating the higher self from being honest and true

Its seduction has choked your logic from the inside out
Soon it will devour your ethos and spit you out with self-doubt

But don't infect me with that nasty parasite inhabiting you
I was once poisoned by its sweet potion of temporary ecstasy too

It has hidden fangs and claws and is known as the ego, a human flaw
So friend, maybe my potion of humility and humor can help you declaw!

Ambrosia

The love Gods refer to it as an elixir behind the third eye

Once excreted, its pleasure takes you beyond any sexual high

There's no wanting or needing anyone's body to be satisfied

This amazing hormonal secretion is the ultimate joyride

When connected to it, you will find self-love and bliss unknown

You'll stop to bitch and moan and forget about ever being blown

Just keep meditating for hours and days without human contact

And this Divine fluid will keep your mind, body and soul intact

Why be so focused on the identity of the physical self they say

Now you'll find pleasure in all people, even ugly and fat everyday

It's known as the ambrosia of life, a beautiful inner ecstasy

Or Amrutha, a Hindu fantasy of immortality

Many East Indians are religiously in hot and anxious pursuit of it

Elevating themselves to a state of pure nirvana to submit

So, this nectar in the pineal gland is well worth experiencing

Too bad that it's against my religion to stop enjoying fucking!

Busy Bees

What has happened to us human busy bees, tell me please

Has life's honey become too bitter to eat and provide a healthy fun release

From popular dance nightclubs to live bars and restaurants

You'll get more talk and show than any real tail to satisfy your wants

A pretty girl's all dressed up in pink and white lace so see through

Yet, she's got no interest in shaking her peaches for a joy ride with you

A handsome guy flaunts his ripped body and has his muscle shirt on

Don't get too excited, his banana is too soft for your wet pussy to hang on

She has the moves to tease men and keep their hungry ego on steroids

He has the balls to play with single lonely women like they're humanoids

Both will be pre-occupied though, comparing each other's fake selfie

It's a new human distraction to make them appear all excited and sexy

So, my friend you might as well get drunk and be stupidly high

Now's a good time to numb yourself below the waist and tell the mind a lie

Because no hottie's opening their beehive and sharing any honey tonight

We've stopped enjoying another person's real flesh and sweet delight

Welcome to a new world of sex naysayers, instead of active pollinators

Yes, the busy bee humans are turning into abstainers and masturbators!

Hourglass Companion

I sit still on your table and I can be activated

Just flip me over and I'll get really animated

I am transparent for your blurred and myopic eyes

But I'm not here to drown your heart and justify your lies

I'm more than a shot glass for you to suck down

Everything starts when you turn me upside down

I'm not here to listen to your sorry ass yesterdays

Just one look at me and you'll change your fearful ways

I'm your earthly liberator that you may not obviously see

To make you more aware and be strong like the roots of a tree

I'm filled with light and high energy goodness

To pour all over you and transform your time of darkness

I am your extraordinary and temporary hourglass companion

Here to shake and awaken you, my ordinary flawed human

I am your ticking time clock to reset your imprisoned reality

A reminder to fill yourself up with love and set your Spirit free!

I'll Keep on Turning

You live each minute, hour and day like you matter
Putting your brain, your heart and your soul in chaotic shatter

You've got this thing about conquering everything
Yet, your fears and rigidity only take you on a downswing

The brain you wear is like a rocket ship with unlimited fire
It knows only how to take off, but not how to retire

The heart you carry is like a door on a spacecraft
It stays mostly closed to avoid any unpleasant downdraft

The soul you harbor is like the damaged mirrors on a satellite
It reflects the dark particles in the void more than the rays of light

You're just an insignificant speck of dust in the vast universe
Yet, you choose to magnify your shit and shrink yourself for worse

You've been created by an unknown higher entity you can't see
And that mystery is mindfucking you, keeping you from being free

But me, I have no such burden, stress or human yearning
I'm just a blue planet with you idiots on board, and I'll keep on turning!

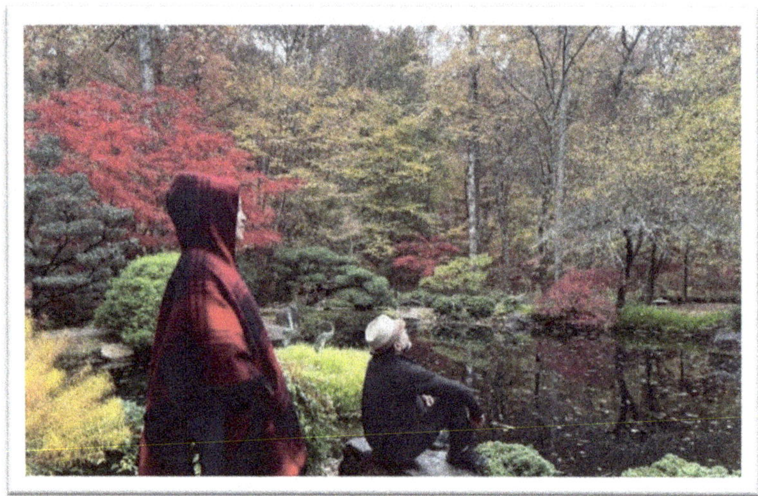

Earth Date: 10.29.2022

On this date, about five weeks after my wife left me, we mutually decided to reconnect in the North Georgia mountains; an idyllic fall setting for both of us to reflect on our 40-year spiritual bond together. I was mentally strong by then and didn't want to spoil this opportunity with woes of our individual breakdowns. My goal was to move forward with forgiveness and drench her with love, laughter and light. That weekend, we danced, bathed in nature, rekindled our love, and stayed in the present. Our getaway reinforced a deep respect and admiration for each other. My wife looked at me and said *"I love you forever,"* but needed to spend more time being alone. I understood and encouraged her to do whatever it takes to get to an *'unfuck'* stage — like I had done for myself. It's not certain how the next chapter of our life unfolds together and what our Creator has planned for us. But whatever the ending, I believe it's been the best love story that any one of us could have conceived, wrote and lived. I know my daughter and son would agree. What an extraordinary ride. I'm not sure about my wife, but I am grateful for *all* of it: the blessing, the breakup, the breakdown and my own breakthrough!

I started out the book by asking the heartbroken lover:

"What the *fuck* now?"

It's a mindfuck, as we crazy humans have the word 'fuck' to mean two opposite things: from a pleasurable sexual intercourse to a painful vulgar act… and everything in-between! And although I meant "What the *pain* now?" to make the title *unfuck* define my dark to light 'transformation,' one can make a case for "What the *pleasure* now?" referring to an oxymoronic viewpoint that is liberating and powerful. So, no matter how you see a breakup, one thing is certain — there are two types of humans you can choose to be; the first is just an 'ordinary' conventional-minded one, who wakes up in the face of any crisis and goes into a victimized fetal posture or a vengeful attack mode, which is disempowering — or the second kind; an '*extra*ordinary' spiritual being who stands tall and goes the 'extra' step by adapting, being self-aware, creative, forgiving, loving, and activating the higher self by saying;

"Thank you, now let me go *unfuck* myself!"

Being this type of *self-responsible* human is the most empowering and your best choice. And in this poetry book, I've shown you through unfiltered self-expression how I not only survived my life's biggest storm, but came out the other side stronger by rebalancing and un-fucking myself from the inside out. And it's highly liberating!

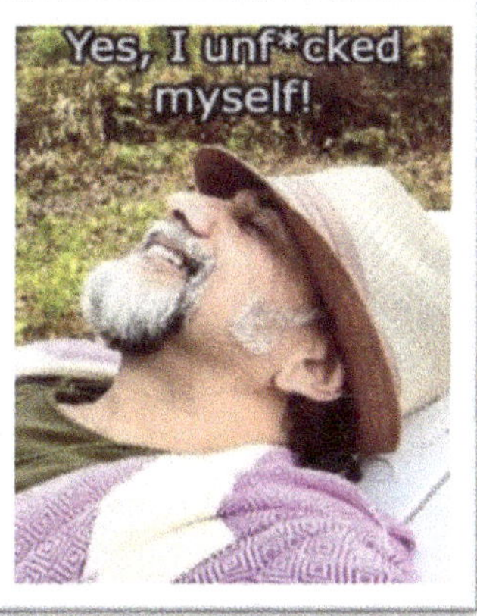

Selfie by Jim Peera

So, now it's time for <u>you</u> to free yourself of your own earthly shit by going above and beyond the ordinary mindset and to just…

<u>GO UNFUCK YOURSELF!</u>

Untitled Bonus Poem...

Here, I want *you* to give it a title and finish it :)

____

Yesterday I was foolish and drove myself insane
I was attached to a restless mind that loved to pull my chain

The night sky above was filled with stars and moonlight
But my eyes saw it to be all stark and out of sight

The morning sun greeted me with a bright smile
Yet, my lips were pouting from being in solitary exile

The water in the shower was hot and steaming
But my cold body was just lifeless and still limping

The truth mirror on the wall kept undressing me once more
It said, I need that sexy love-machine back that I adore

Life is too short to waste it feeding the virus in your head
It's time to come alive and make some magic memories in bed

So today I am wiser, lighter and free from those days forgone
And to always be grateful for having a nice fucking...

___________________!

Fill in the blank

"Each day you have a choice to look at life for how others see it

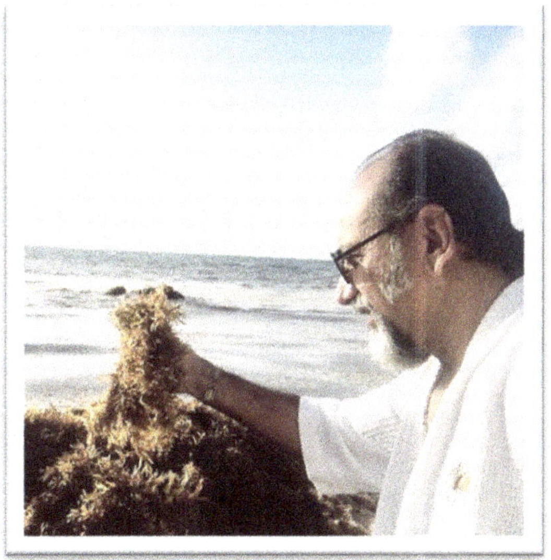

Or for how YOU can seize it!"

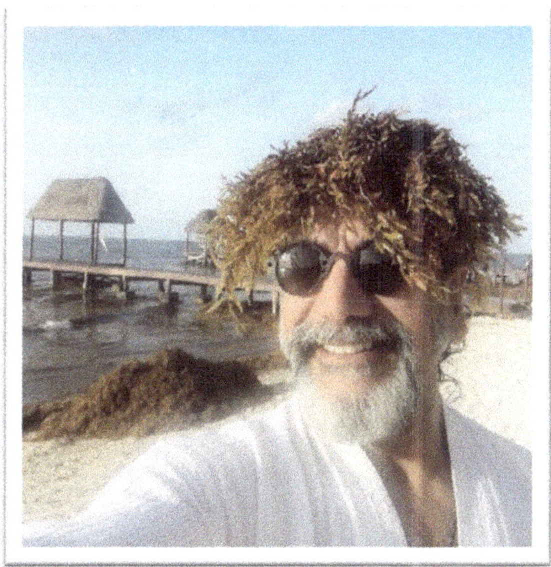

Quote and Selfie by Jim Peera

Some of my favorite quotes:

"Have a mind that's open to everything and attached to nothing."

— Dr. Wayne Dyer

"The effect you have on others is the most valuable currency there is."

— Jim Carrey

"Art is a wound turned into light."

— Georges Braque

"Don't sweat the petty things and don't pet the sweaty things."

— George Carlin

"Life is a balance between holding on and letting go."

— Rumi

"Instead of looking for a person who checks all the boxes, focus on a person with whom you can imagine yourself writing a story with, that entails edits and revisions."

— Esther Perel

Also, by Jim Peera…

A captivating MEMOIR, a no-nonsense SELF-HELP GUIDE and a creative PEACE PLAN FOR AMERICA!

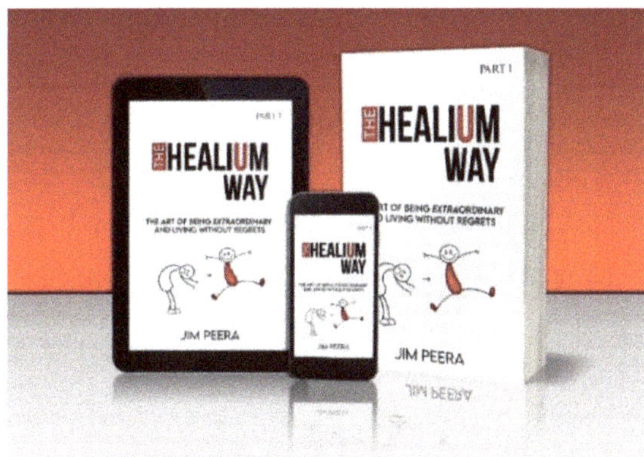

The Healium Way - Part 1

An Interactive and exciting book filled with art, poetry, exercises and amazing real-life stories.

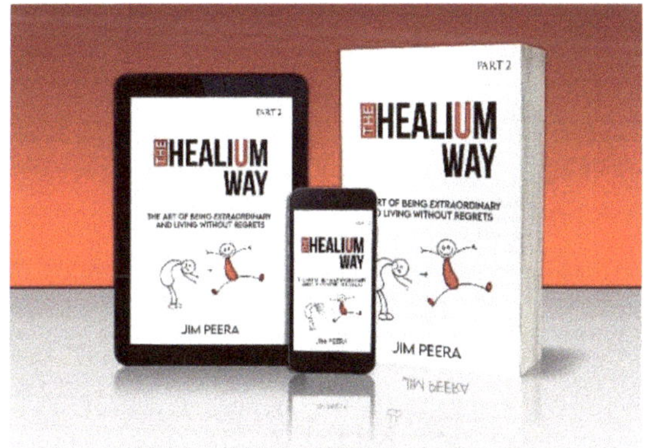

The Healium Way - Part 2

"Read this book and get *Healiumized!*"

TheHealiumWay.com

"LIVE Like Your Body Won't Get Up Tomorrow
LAUGH Like Your Mind is Sick of Sorrow
LOVE Like Your Heart is Just for Borrow."

- Jim Peera

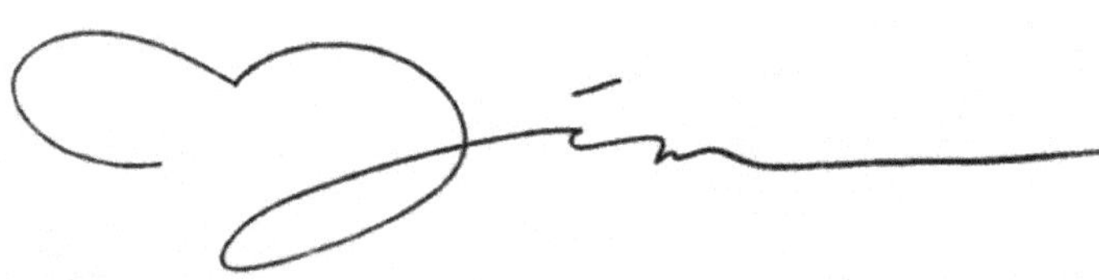

About the Author

Jim Peera (born Azim Peera), has been called a renaissance man. He's a non-conformist creative, accomplished entrepreneur, inventor, real-estate developer, surrealist sculptor, healer, author, poet, world traveler, a lover of life, and a warrior of peace.

He founded the nonprofit interactive wellness-with-the-arts center; Healium Center in Atlanta, Georgia in 2014 and published his 2-part book "The Healium Way: The art of being extraordinary and living without regrets." in 2022.

Jim has lived a full and adventurous life and his journey hasn't been short of being extraordinary. Through the good, the bad and the ugly, Jim has always believed in living a life of balance with the medicine of the creative and healing arts as his drug of choice. In addition to sculpting, photography, and drumming; poetry has always been his favorite therapy for self-expression and healing.

The multi-dimensional American immigrant from Tanzania, East Africa is a down-to-earth spiritual family man with two grown children and a wife of forty years. He has lived in France, England, Costa Rica and currently lives in the U.S A.

For more information visit him at JimPeera.com